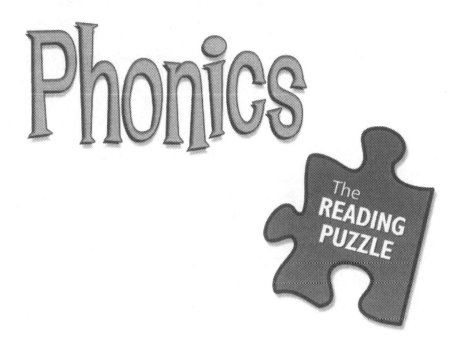

Phonics

The
**READING
PUZZLE**

Elaine K. McEwan

Michelle Judware
Darlene Carino
Candace Darling

CORWIN PRESS
Classroom

For information:

Corwin Press
A SAGE Company
2455 Teller Road
Thousand Oaks, California 91320
CorwinPress.com

SAGE, Ltd.
1 Oliver's Yard
55 City Road
London EC1Y 1SP
United Kingdom

SAGE India Pvt. Ltd.
B 1/I 1 Mohan Cooperative
Industrial Area
Mathura Road, New Delhi
India 110 044

SAGE Asia-Pacific Pvt. Ltd.
33 Pekin Street #02-01
Far East Square
Singapore 048763

ISBN: 978-1-4129-5821-9

This book is printed on acid-free paper.

08 09 10 11 12 10 9 8 7 6 5 4 3 2 1

Executive Editor: Kathleen Hex
Managing Developmental Editor: Christine Hood
Editorial Assistant: Anne O'Dell
Developmental Writers: Michelle Judware, Darlene Carino, Candace Darling
Developmental Editor: Carolea Williams
Proofreader: Carrie Reiling
Art Director: Anthony D. Paular
Design Project Manager: Jeffrey Stith
Cover Designers: Michael Dubowe and Jeffrey Stith
Illustrator: Ben Mahan
Design Consultant: The Development Source

Phonics

The READING PUZZLE

TABLE OF CONTENTS

Introduction

Students must be taught the relationship between phonemes (language sounds) and graphemes (written letters) in order to decode words. Understanding this relationship between letters and their respective sounds is vital to reading success and is a key element in reading instruction. Literacy is dependent on students' mastery of letter-sound correspondences.

Research has proven that students who are directly instructed in the alphabetic principle improve in their word-reading skills at a significantly higher rate than students who only indirectly receive phonics instruction. The activities in this resource are presented in a logical order that will help you deliver explicit and systematic phonics instruction for:

- Consonants

- Short vowels and long vowels

- Consonant blends and digraphs

- Sight words

- Compound words

One of the greatest challenges all educators face is the struggle to capture and hold the interest and attention of students. This resource offers many engaging and stimulating activities to teach students how to discern the similarities and differences between letters and sounds. The activities include chants and games that will motivate students and encourage them to practice and further develop their phonics skills.

The activities also address different learning styles to meet the needs of all students. They can be used during whole-group or small-group instruction as well as in independent learning stations. Also included are many ready-to-use reproducibles that require very little preparation. These will help give you more teaching time planning for and providing differentiated instruction.

The content in *Phonics K–3* not only provides an explicit and systematic course of instruction, but also offers high-interest activities to keep students on target. Phonics instruction is a key foundation for learning to read and is necessary to instill a lifelong love reading in your students that paves the way to academic achievement and success.

Put It Into Practice

Once students have acquired solid phonemic awareness skills, they are ready to add the piece of the Reading Puzzle that enables them to rapidly and fluently identify words: phonics. Phonics is the "body of knowledge about the relationship between written and spoken words, skill in its use, and a positive attitude toward its application in reading and writing" (Chall, 1996).

Strategies used to teach phonics are an important part of the Reading Puzzle. The Reading Puzzle is a way of organizing and understanding reading instruction, as introduced in my book, *Teach Them All to Read: Catching the Kids Who Fall Through the Cracks* (2002). The puzzle contains the essential reading skills that students need to master in order to become literate at every grade level. *The Reading Puzzle, Grades K–3* series focuses on five of these skills: Vocabulary, Comprehension, Fluency, Phonemic Awareness, and Phonics.

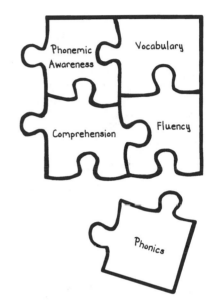

When students understand the "phonics code," they can quickly decode (i.e., sound out any new words they encounter). Although I do not speak Spanish fluently, I do know the Spanish code, so I can correctly pronounce Spanish words. During reading, successful readers employ one or more of the following strategies to help in decoding:

- Analyze and blend together individual phonemes

- Notice and blend together familiar spelling patterns involving more than one letter

- Make analogies to other words that they already know (Ehri, 1998)

During a first encounter with any new word, skilled readers phonologically recode the phonetic structure of the word into memory, as well as the movements of their mouth, lips, and tongue during its pronunciation. So, when the word is encountered again, they can accurately retrieve the sounds and read the word more rapidly than was possible the first time.

I would advise anyone who has wondered about the research relative to phonics instruction to read it for themselves—not just take someone else's word for what a study might say. I recommend two studies for your consideration: The First-Grade Studies (Bond & Dykstra, 1967) and The Houston Study (Foorman, Fletcher, Francis, Schatschneider, & Mehta, 1998). Their findings, considered along with such comprehensive reviews of the research as Adams (1990), Chall (1967/1983), the National Reading Panel (2000), and the National Research Council (Snow, et al., 1998), should leave no doubt in your mind about the critical role phonics plays in beginning reading instruction. Explicit, systematic, supportive phonics instruction, taught as a stand-alone instructional component within the context of a print-rich classroom environment with a significant literature base, is an absolutely essential (although certainly not sufficient) piece of the Reading Puzzle—particularly for at-risk learners.

The First-Grade Studies found that reading programs containing "stronger, more systematic phonics components" produced better results in reading achievement at the end of first grade (Bond & Dykstra, 1967). The Houston Study found that students who were directly instructed in the alphabetic principle improved in word-reading skill at a significantly faster rate than students indirectly instructed in the alphabetic principle through exposure to literature (Foorman, et al., 1998).

Principals and teachers who have seen dramatic increases in literacy attainment in low-performing schools have used precisely the kind of direct code instruction found to be most effective in the Foorman study (Antrim, 2001; Carter, 1999; Dobberteen, 2001; King & Torgesen, 2000; Kollars, 1999; McEwan, 1998, 2001). These instructional leaders know that without a foundation of phonics, the majority of their students would still be "falling through the cracks."

Successful teachers and principals also know, however, that phonics is only one piece of the Reading Puzzle. Without ongoing instruction in cognitive strategies, the continual development of language skills, the deepening of knowledge through solid content-area instruction, voluminous reading in all types of text, and daily opportunities to talk and write about what is read using the conventions of spoken and written language, any gains realized in kindergarten and first grade will disappear by the upper grades. Conversely, without a phonics foundation, students will not even have the option of becoming literate (Foorman, Fletcher, Francis, & Schatschneider, 2000).

CHAPTER 1

Cruising with Consonants

Alphabet Soup

Begin cooking up some excitement with this alphabet activity. Set up a "consonant cooking kitchen" in a special section of your classroom. Set out a soup pot, a stirring spoon, and a chef's hat and apron.

1. Choose a consonant to highlight over a two-day period. On the first day, ask students to bring in items that begin with the target consonant. Tell students that their items will be combined together to make a delicious "alphabet soup."

2. Gather students in the consonant cooking kitchen. Ask one student to hold up his or her item. Invite him or her to name the beginning sound as you write the name of the item on a sentence strip.

3. Have students clap out and chant the letters in the word. Then, with students, count to three and drop the item into your special alphabet soup pot!

4. Repeat Steps 2 and 3 until all students have added their "ingredients" to the soup.

5. Display all the words that begin with the target consonant on a bulletin board titled *Special Ingredients*. Have students reread the words aloud. Underline the beginning consonant to check whether the item belongs in this special pot of alphabet soup.

6. Before you begin this activity on the second day, secretly hide in the bottom of the soup pot a special treat that begins with the target letter. (See Magical Treats suggestions on page 8.)

7. On the second day, invite a student to be the "soup chef." Have this student wear the chef's apron and hat. Ask the chef to tap the side of the pot three times as the class says the "Alphabet Soup" chant:

Alphabet Soup

*Here's the letter **d***
To make our soup pot bubble!
We know its special sound,
*Let's say it on the double: **/d/ /d/ /d/**.*
Shout out the magic words—
Alakazam, Alakazoop!
Our magic is done,
So dish up some soup!

After students complete the chant, have the chef pull each ingredient from the pot and return it to its owner. Invite the chef to hold up the magical treat revealed underneath all the items. Ask the chef to hand out the treats!

Magical Treats

You can purchase many of these items in discount stores and party supply stores. You can also order many of them in bulk from incentive catalogs and online.

B–bouncy balls, bookmarks

C–cookies

D–"dog" erasers

F–mini-flags

G–goody bags

H–happy face stamps, toy horses

J–joke books, jets

K–key chains

L–lollipops

M–movie passes, tiny toy mice

N–necklaces, noisemakers

P–number puzzles, finger puppets, pinwheels

Q–quiet toys

R–rings, ring pops

S–stickers, spiders

T–toothbrushes

V–video time

W–whistles

X–extra playtime coupons

Y–yo-yos

Z–zoo animal pencils

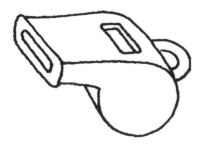

978-1-4129-5821-9

Mixed-Up Letters

Letters most commonly mixed up by young students in the primary grades are the lowercase letters *b*, *d*, *p*, and *q*. Similarities between these letters make it difficult for students to identify them quickly and accurately.

1. Copy the **b**, **d**, **p**, and **q letter reproducibles (pages 10–13)**. Color the letter posters and display them on a small bulletin board titled *Print Your Letters Carefully*. These posters engage a variety of learning styles by offering visual and auditory clues for correct letter formation.

2. Recite the following letter poem for students to begin the lesson:

Mixed-Up Letter Poem

> *b* meets *d* and says, "Oh, gee!
> You seem to look a lot like me."
> Next, *p* walks by and says, "Hee, hee, hee!
> I look a lot like *b* and *d*."
> Then, *q* comes by and says, "Goodness me!
> I look a lot like **b**, **d**, **p**."
> Let's keep their true identity
> By printing them so carefully!

3. Introduce the letter *b*. Display the *b* letter poster on the bulletin board. Read the poem aloud, modeling on the poster how to form the letter *b*. Invite students to draw the letter in the air as you read.

4. Introduce the letters *d*, *p*, and *q* in the same way. Read the poem on each letter poster, inviting students to draw the letter in the air. Remind students that they can refer to the posters while they read or write.

First the hockey stick,
And then the puck.
Now you've formed a "b"
With any luck!

Reproducible

978-1-4129-5821-9 • © Corwin Press

Make a "c,"
Climb up the tree.
That's the way
You make a "d."

A long, long stem
Goes underground.
A pretty flower circles 'round.

This letter is so clear to see,
This letter is a pretty "p."

Reproducible   978-1-4129-5821-9 • © Corwin Press

The "q" coaster circles back,
Climbs up,
Slides down,
And off the track!

Reproducible *The Reading Puzzle: Phonics • Grades K–3* **13**

Mind Your Ps and Qs

The purpose of this game is to provide students with many opportunities to quickly and accurately identify four lowercase letters (*b, d, p, q*). These letters are often confused because of their visual similarities.

1. Make a copy of the **Letter Race Game Board** and **Letter Cards reproducibles (pages 15–16)** for each group of two or three players. Cut out the letter cards. Direct each group to place the cards facedown in a stack by the game board. Give each player a small button to use as a game piece.

2. Have each player place a game piece at the *START* position on the game board. Invite students to take turns drawing a card from the pile and reading the letter on it. Point out that each letter card has a line on it. Model how to hold the letter card with the line at the bottom in order to read the letter correctly. This will help prevent students from mixing up letters (e.g., *d* and *p*).

3. After a player reads a letter card, have him or her move the game piece to the first matching letter on the game board. For example, if a player draws a *p* letter card, he or she would move to the first *p* on the game board.

4. Players continue to draw cards and make their way around the game board. The first player in each group to reach the finish line is the winner!

Monitor students to be sure they are placing their game pieces on the correct letters. If a player moves to an incorrect space, he or she must go back to the beginning of the race.

978-1-4129-5821-9

Letter Race Game Board

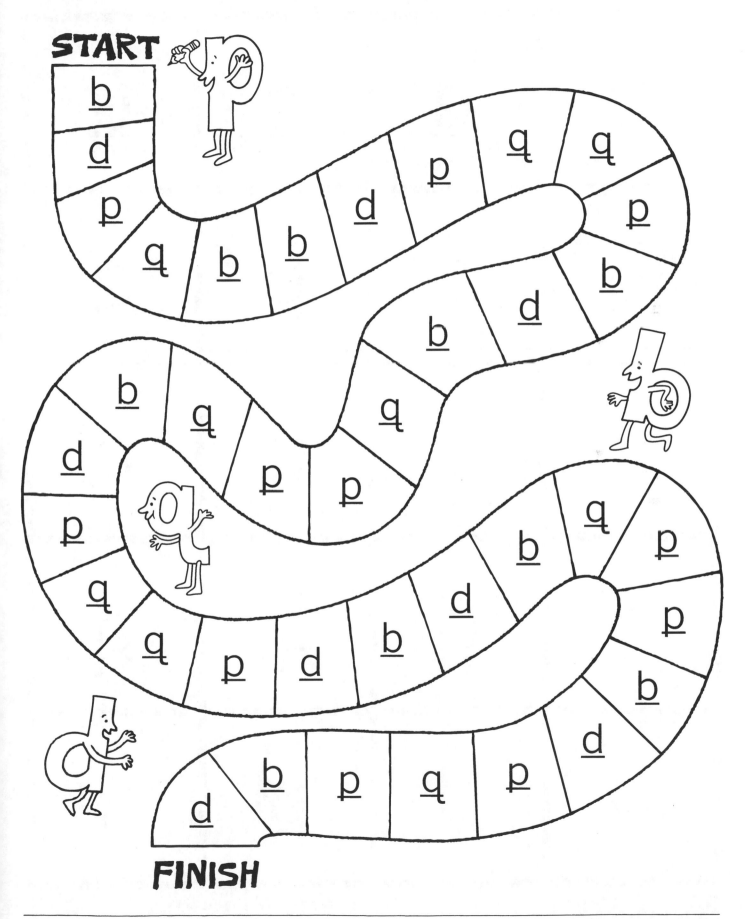

START

FINISH

Letter Cards

b	d	p	q
b	d	p	q
b	d	p	q
b	d	p	q
b	d	p	q

Reproducible

Slither 'Round

1. Write each uppercase consonant on one end of a craft stick. On each of five craft sticks, draw a snake slithering up the stick.

2. Decorate the outside of a juice can to look like a snake's den. Place all of the craft sticks in the "den" so the ends with letters on them are at the bottom of the can.

3. Have students stand in a circle. Explain to them that inside the den are five sleeping snakes. The snakes are snuggled up with uppercase consonant letters. The students' job is to "rescue" the letters without disturbing any of the snakes.

4. Pass the container around the circle. Have each student slide one stick out of the container without looking inside. If the stick has a letter on it, the student must say the name of the letter. If the student identifies the letter correctly, he or she keeps the stick. The letter is now rescued! If the student does not know the letter, say the name of the letter for him or her. Then have the student slide the stick back in the snake's den.

5. If a student draws a stick with a snake on it, all students holding letter sticks must return them to the can! Have the class chant the "Slitherin' Snakes" poem while slithering around the circle like snakes:

Slitherin' Snakes

See them! Say them! Slither 'round!

Here are letters we have found: ___, ___, ___, . . .

(Have students name the letters that have been drawn so far.)

Silly snakes don't make a sound,

But drag our letters underground.

Place all the sticks back in the container and continue to play the game. For a variation, play the game with lowercase letters or sound spellings.

Consonant Collage

Literacy is dependent on students' mastery of letter-sound correspondences. In this activity, each student will focus on the sound of one letter by creating a consonant collage.

1. Explain to students that a collage is a collection of items arranged to form artwork. Tell students that they will gather pictures to create a consonant collage.

2. Make several copies of the **Alphabet Cards reproducibles (pages 22–28)**. Cut out the cards and separate the consonants from the vowels. (Store the vowel cards that you will not be using for this activity in an envelope. Glue the storage label from the reproducible on page 28 to the front of the envelope. You will use these alphabet cards for several activities that follow.)

3. Give each student a different consonant letter card (uppercase, lowercase, or both) and a sheet of construction paper.

4. Invite each student to make a consonant collage of his or her assigned letter by cutting pictures from magazines that begin with the same letter. After students have cut out appropriate pictures, direct them to glue the pictures and letter card to a sheet of construction paper.

5. Display the consonant collages or bind them together to make a consonant dictionary.

   978-1-4129-5821-9

Memory Match-Up

This game challenges students to use their knowledge of letter-sound correspondences as well as their memories.

1. Make several copies of the Alphabet Cards reproducibles (pages 22–28) or use the cards you have already prepared and stored in an envelope from the "Consonant Collage" activity (page 18).

2. Prepare a set of ten letter cards (uppercase or lowercase) and ten matching picture cards for each pair of students. Place each set of cards in a resealable plastic bag.

3. Give each pair of students a bag of cards. Tell students that they will be matching each letter card with a picture that starts with the same sound.

4. Invite students to spread out the cards facedown in a grid pattern on a table. Have the first player turn over two cards. If the cards match, the player keeps the cards and continues to turn over two cards at a time until he or she can no longer make a match. If the cards do not match, the player turns the cards back over, and the next player takes a turn.

5. Players must use their memory skills to recall cards that have been revealed and then turned back over in order to successfully find letter-sound matches. The player with the most matches wins!

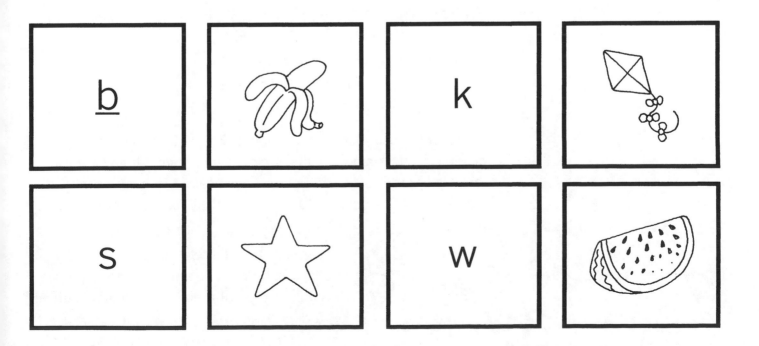

Little Letter Line-Up

Alphabetical order is an essential skill that proves especially helpful for word study, conducting research, and organizing information. This activity will appeal to kinesthetic learners as players move around the room to practice their alphabetizing skills.

1. Make copies of the Alphabet Cards reproducibles (pages 22–28) and cut out the cards. You will use only the uppercase letters as you begin this activity. (Or, use the Alphabet Cards you have already prepared and stored in an envelope from a previous activity.)

2. Have students stand in a circle on the rug. Explain to the class that a group of letters has gotten very mixed up. These letters do not know anyone around them. Tell students that to help out, they need to arrange the letters in order as quickly as possible so the letters are back near their friends.

3. Give each student an uppercase letter card. If there are fewer than 26 students in the class, give some students two consecutive cards, such as *A* and *B* or *Y* and *Z*.

4. Invite students to arrange themselves in alphabetical order by finding the letters that should be on either side of them. Tell students to remember that to be quick, there can be no talking.

5. Once students have silently arranged themselves from *A* to *Z*, recite the "Letter Line-Up" poem.

Letter Line-Up

> *Letters, letters A to Z,*
>
> *Hold your letters so all can see.*
>
> *Say them, say them, one, two, three.*
>
> *Say your letters A to Z!*

6. If students need more practice identifying letters, invite them to say their letters aloud as they hold up their cards. If any letters are out of order, say: *Try it, try it once again. Make sure each letter has a friend!* Encourage students to silently fix their letter line-up.

7. Vary this activity! Use the lowercase letter cards or the alphabet picture cards. Try using a timer to see how quickly students can silently put themselves in alphabetical order. Challenge each student to say a word that begins with the letter he or she is holding.

978-1-4129-5821-9

Mother, May I Say?

1. Make a copy of the Alphabet Cards reproducibles (pages 22–28) and cut out the cards. (Or, use the Alphabet Cards you have already prepared and stored in an envelope from a previous activity.) Place the uppercase letters facedown in a stack in the center of a playing area.

2. Choose a student to go first. That player draws a letter card from the stack. Then the player rolls a die to determine how many words he or she must say that begin with the letter on the card. The student then says: *Mother, may I say _____ words that begin with _____? For example: Mother, may I say **four** words that begin with **p**?* (pig, pickles, pink, Paul)

3. Award students who are able to think of the correct number of words beginning with the target letter sound the corresponding number of points. If a student cannot think of enough words beginning with the target letter sound, do not award any points. The player with the most points wins!

Tickle Me Alphabet

1. Divide the class into groups of two. Let groups find quiet places around the classroom to sit. Be sure that partners are comfortable working together.

2. Make several copies of the Alphabet Cards reproducibles (pages 22–28) and cut out the cards. (Or, use the Alphabet Cards you have already prepared and stored in an envelope from a previous activity.) Give each pair of students a set of uppercase or lowercase letters and two craft sticks. Have partners place the stack of alphabet cards facedown in a pile.

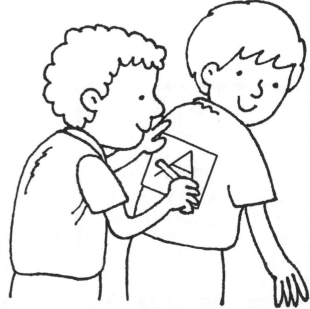

3. Explain to students that they will be using craft sticks to "tickle" or trace a letter on their partner's back. If the partner is able to guess the letter, tell the sound it makes, and say a word that begins with that letter, he or she can keep the card. If the partner cannot identify the letter correctly and provide the sound and a sample word, the student who traced the letter places the card back in the pile. The player with the most letter cards at the end of the game is the "Tickle Me Alphabet" champion!

Alphabet Cards

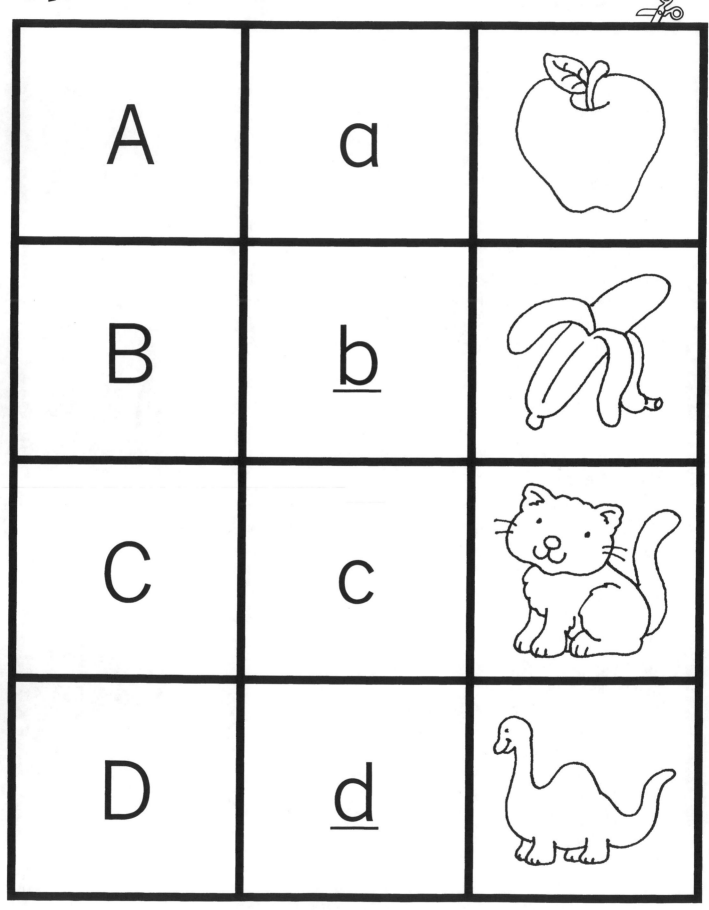

A	a	(apple)
B	<u>b</u>	(banana)
C	c	(cat)
D	<u>d</u>	(dinosaur)

Reproducible   978-1-4129-5821-9 • © Corwin Press

Alphabet Cards

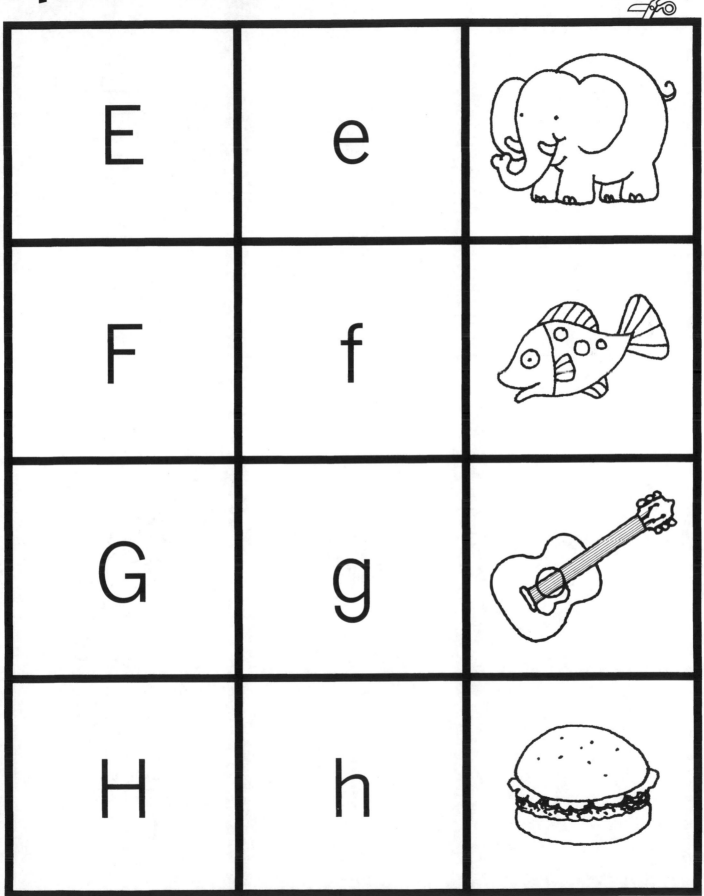

Alphabet Cards

I	i	
J	j	
K	k	
L	l	

Alphabet Cards

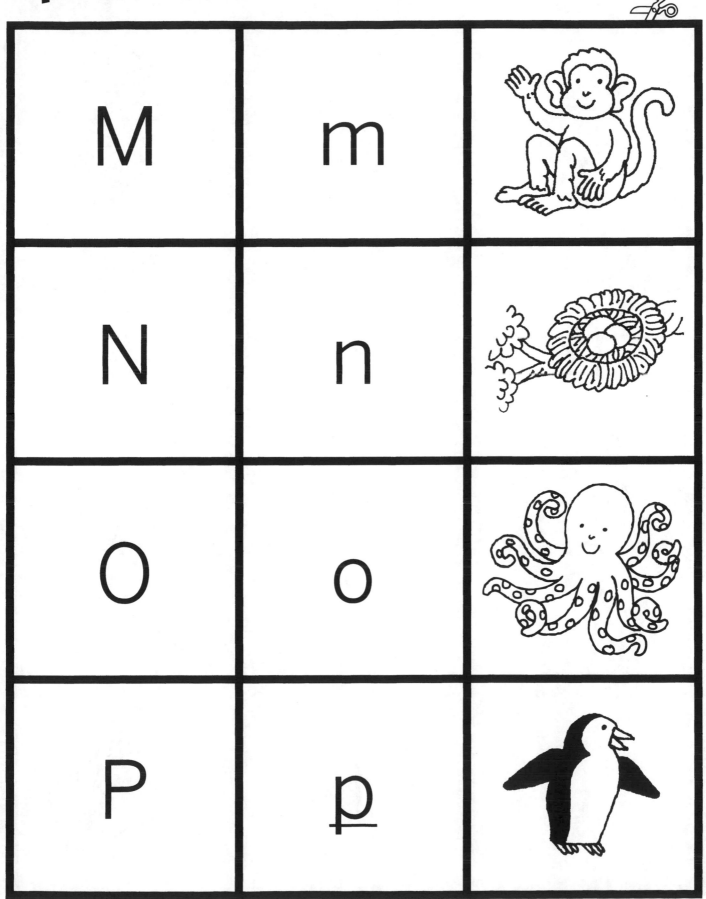

M	m	🐵
N	n	🪹
O	o	🐙
P	p	🐧

Alphabet Cards

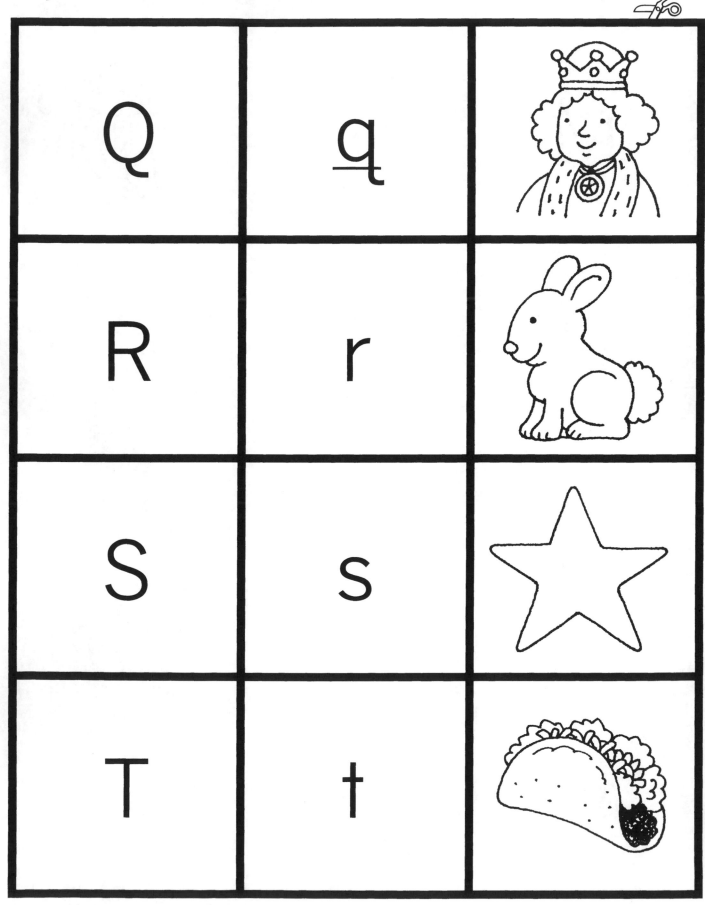

Q	q	
R	r	
S	s	
T	t	

Reproducible 978-1-4129-5821-9 • © Corwin Press

Alphabet Cards

U	u	
V	v	
W	w	
X	x	

Alphabet Cards

Y	y	
Z	z	

Alphabet Cards A B C

Reproducible

978-1-4129-5821-9 • © Corwin Press

The Grocery Game

Letter-sound correspondence knowledge is a prerequisite to effective word identification. In this activity, students will use their imagination, knowledge of letter sounds, and alphabetical order skills to play a fun memory game.

1. Invite students to sit in a circle on the rug. Explain that they are going to go grocery shopping at the Consonant Corner Store.

2. Begin the activity by choosing a grocery item for the first consonant, *b*. For example, say: *Before we go to the Consonant Corner Store, we need to list groceries that we want to buy. Let's begin with me. I'm going to the Consonant Corner Store, and I want to buy some* **butter**.

3. Write the word *butter* on chart paper to begin a grocery list. Underline the beginning consonant.

4. Choose a student to continue the activity by thinking of a grocery item that begins with the next consonant letter, *c*. Add each student's grocery item to the list on the chart paper and underline the beginning consonant. Going around the circle, invite each student to add a grocery item to the list by saying the name of an item that begins with the next consonant letter, in alphabetical order. Continue until an item is listed for each consonant.

5. Vary the activity by playing "Before or After." Begin with any letter of the alphabet and call out *before* or *after*. Students need to think of a grocery item that begins with the letter that comes before or after the letter you called. For example, if you say: *M, before,* students need to name a grocery item that begins with the letter *L*.

6. Another way to vary the activity is to play "Zoobaloo." Invite students to name zoo animals using each initial consonant sound.

CHAPTER 2

A Galaxy of Vowels

Short-Vowel Sounds We Love to Say

Vowel sounds can be more difficult for students to master because each vowel letter represents two different vowel sounds—long and short. Use the following poems to capture students' attention when introducing each new short-vowel sound.

1. Write each poem on chart paper and read it aloud to students.

2. Invite students to help you highlight words in each poem that contains the target short-vowel sound. Chant the poems several times along with students. Call on students to help brainstorm a list of short-vowel words to go along with each poem.

Short A

*Short **a** is the sound*

We love to snap

*In **clap** and **strap**.*

/ă/ /ă/ /ă/

*Short **a** is the sound*

We love to add

*To **mad** and **bad**.*

*Short **a** is such a little sound.*

Say /ă/ /ă/ /ă/

*When **a** is around.*

Short E

*Short **e** is the sound*

We love to pet

*In **wet** and **set**.*

/ĕ/ /ĕ/ /ĕ/

*Short **e** is the sound*

We love to spell

*In **fell** and **bell**.*

*Short **e** is such a little sound.*

Say /ĕ/ /ĕ/ /ĕ/

*When **e** is around.*

Short I

Short *i* is the sound

We love to win

In **fin** and **pin**.

/ĭ/ /ĭ/ /ĭ/

Short *i* is the sound

We love to fill

In **mill** and **bill**.

Short *i* is such a little sound.

Say /ĭ/ /ĭ/ /ĭ/

When *i* is around.

Short O

Short *o* is the sound

We love a lot

In **hot** and **got**.

/ŏ/ /ŏ/ /ŏ/

Short *o* is a sound

We love to pop

In **hop** and **mop**.

Short *o* is such a little sound.

Say /ŏ/ /ŏ/ /ŏ/

When *o* is around.

Short U

Short *u* is the sound

We love to hug

In **bug** and **mug**.

/ŭ/ /ŭ/ /ŭ/

Short *u* is the sound

We love for fun

In **sun** and **run**.

Short *u* is such a little sound.

Say /ŭ/ /ŭ/ /ŭ/

When *u* is around.

Long Vowel Name-O

After students master short-vowel sounds using the previous activities, introduce these long-vowel activities. It is important for students to master short-vowel sounds before moving on to long-vowel sounds. However, the following activities can be used with either short-vowel or long-vowel words.

1. Use the following songs, sung to the tune of "Bingo," to introduce each vowel sound. Write each song on chart paper. Sing the songs several times with students.

2. Invite students to brainstorm new words to add to each verse. Write the words on sticky notes. Place the sticky notes on the chart paper as you sing the new version.

Long A

There was a vowel

Who said its name,

*And long **a** was its name-o.*

*/ā/ /ā/ /ā/ in **day**,*

*/ā/ /ā/ /ā/ in **bay**,*

*/ā/ /ā/ /ā/ in **clay**,*

*And long **a** was its name-o.*

Long E

There was a vowel

Who said its name,

*And long **e** was its name-o.*

*/ē/ /ē/ /ē/ in **see**,*

*/ē/ /ē/ /ē/ in **me**,*

*/ē/ /ē/ /ē/ in **key**,*

*And long **e** was its name-o.*

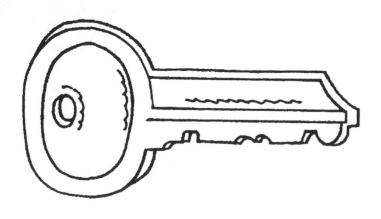

978-1-4129-5821-9

Long I

There was a vowel
Who said its name,
And long *i* was its name-o.
/ī/ /ī/ /ī/ in **pie**,
/ī/ /ī/ /ī/ in **tie**,
/ī/ /ī/ /ī/ in **high**,
And long *i* was its name-o.

Long O

There was a vowel
Who said its name,
And long *o* was its name-o.
/ō/ /ō/ /ō/ in **soap**,
/ō/ /ō/ /ō/ in **road**,
/ō/ /ō/ /ō/ in **toad**,
And long *o* was its name-o.

Long U

There was a vowel
Who said its name,
And long *u* was its name-o.
/ū/ /ū/ /ū/ in **mule**,
/ū/ /ū/ /ū/ in **rule**,
/ū/ /ū/ /ū/ in **fuel**,
And long *u* was its name-o.

Food Fight

1. Explain to students that the short-vowel letters are in a terrible argument about which foods taste the best. Of course, short *a* thinks that foods with the /ă/ sound taste best. Short *e* likes foods with the /ĕ/ sound best, and the other vowels like foods with their own vowel sounds. The vowels are in a food fight! They are shouting their sounds and throwing food. When their teacher arrives, she tells the short vowels: *Clean up this mess! Return each food to the vowel that threw it.* Since this is a very big job, the vowels are asking students to help them.

2. Place students in small groups. Make copies of the **Short-Vowel Food Pictures** and **Short-Vowel Lunch Boxes reproducibles (pages 35–36)** for each group. Cut out the cards and lunch boxes before distributing them. Have students place the lunch boxes in a row on a work surface. Invite group members to take turns choosing one short-vowel picture card and placing it underneath the correct short-vowel lunch box.

3. Repeat the activity another time using the **Long-Vowel Food Pictures** and **Long-Vowel Lunch Boxes reproducibles (pages 37–38)**.

Connect Five

1. Tell students that to play the game "Connect Five," they will need to connect five short-vowel words together. Each player must write a word and identify its short-vowel sound.

2. Divide the class into two teams. Have the first student from each team write a short-vowel word on the board. Direct each player to read his or her word to the class and identify its short-vowel sound.

3. Instruct the next player on each team to write a word that begins with the last letter of the previous word. Continue playing until one team is able to create a string a five words—each beginning with the last sound of the previous word, and each having a different short-vowel sound. For example, a team may create the following string of five short-vowel words: *set, tub, beg, gas, sob.*

4. The first team that is able to connect words containing all five vowel sounds shouts: *Connect five!*

978-1-4129-5821-9

Short-Vowel Food Pictures

h__m

c__ndy

__pple

l__mon

__ggs

l__ttuce

ch__cken

ch__ps

h__td__g

p__pcorn

n__ts

s__ndae

Short-Vowel Lunch Boxes

Short A

Short E

Short I

Short O

Short U

978-1-4129-5821-9 • © Corwin Press

Long-Vowel Food Pictures

gr__pes

c__ke

b__con

ch__ese

p__ach

p__e

r__ce

p__neapple

d__nut

__atmeal

c__cumber

j__ice

Long-Vowel Lunch Boxes

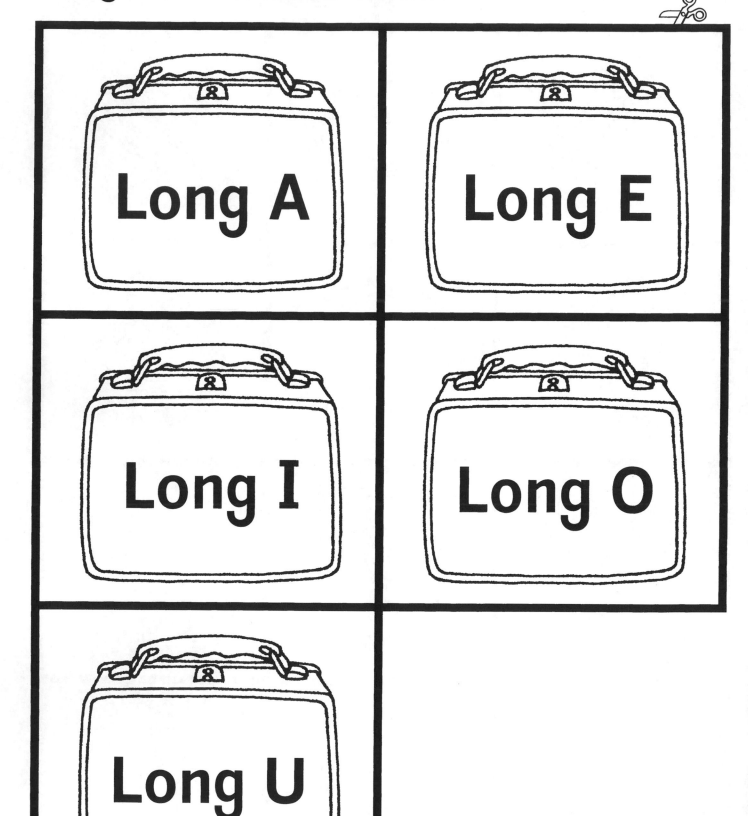

Long A

Long E

Long I

Long O

Long U

Reproducible

Scoop It Up

1. Place students in groups of five. Make enough copies of the **Ice-Cream Cones reproducible (page 40)**, so you can cut out the cones and give each student one cone.

2. Make several copies of the **Ice-Cream Scoops reproducible (page 41)** on different colors of paper. Cut out and give each student three different-colored ice-cream scoops. Explain that each student is going to build a three-scoop ice-cream cone by finding three picture cards that match the vowel on his or her cone.

3. To reinforce vowel sounds, reproduce the **Short-Vowel Picture Cards** and **Long-Vowel Picture Cards reproducibles (pages 42–45)**. Cut out the cards and place them in a stack for each group. Invite students to take turns drawing a card from the stack. If the vowel on the picture card matches the vowel on his or her ice-cream cone, the student can add a scoop on the cone. If it does not, the student must return the picture to the bottom of the stack. Students can use their cones to collect either long-vowel or short-vowel words. For example, if a student has the cone labeled *A*, he or she can collect long *a* or short *a* words. But all the words must have the same vowel sound. The first student to build a three-scoop ice-cream cone wins!

4. Challenge students to build cones with two or four scoops or to play with only the long-vowel or short-vowel cards at one time.

5. As an alternative, let students play this game in pairs. Make a copy of the Ice-Cream Cones reproducible for each student. Explain that one student will look for short-vowel pictures to build scoops on each cone, and his or her partner will look for long-vowel pictures. The first player to build all five cones wins. Challenge students to build two-, three-, or four-scoop cones.

Ice-Cream Cones

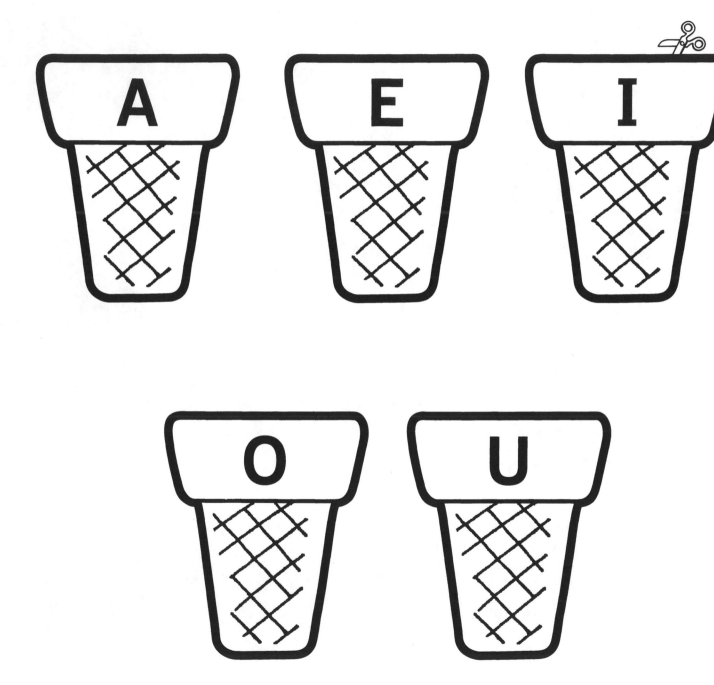

Ice-Cream Scoops

Short-Vowel Picture Cards

c__t	m__n	l__mp
h__t	__nt	sl__d
n__st	b__d	dr__ss
w__b	p__g	f__sh

978-1-4129-5821-9 • © Corwin Press

Short-Vowel Picture Cards

p__n

sh__p

s__ck

d__ll

fr__g

cl__ck

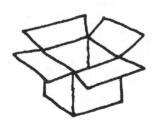

b__x

d__ck

g__m

sk__nk

b__g

c__p

Long-Vowel Picture Cards

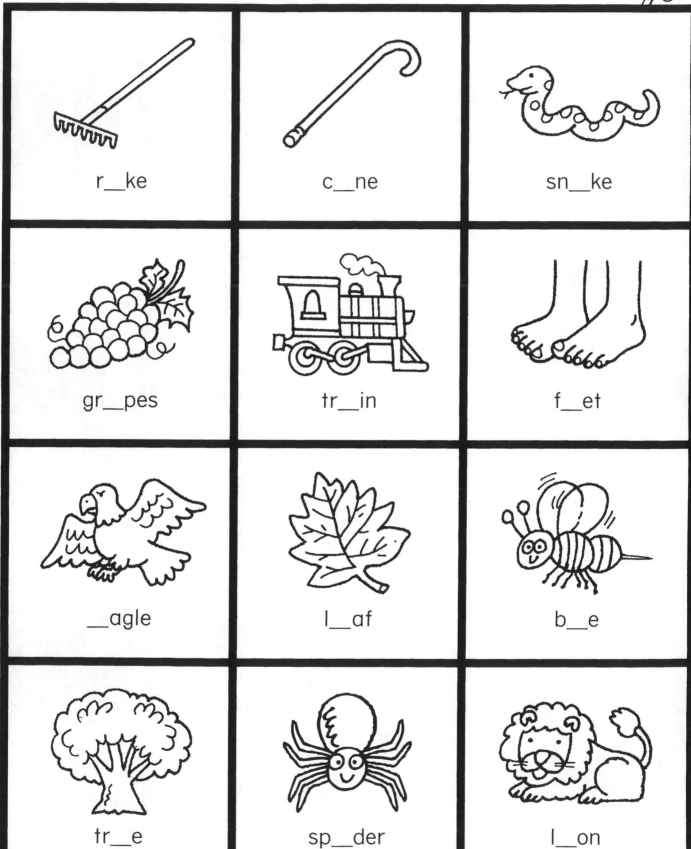

r__ke

c__ne

sn__ke

gr__pes

tr__in

f__et

__agle

l__af

b__e

tr__e

sp__der

l__on

Long-Vowel Picture Cards

d__nosaur

f__ve

k__te

c__at

r__se

r__pe

r__ad

b__at

m__le

fl__te

r__ler

m__sic

Baby Talk

As students become better readers, it is sometimes difficult to tell whether they have really mastered their short-vowel sounds or if they have simply increased their sight vocabulary. This game can be used as a quick and easy short-vowel check.

1. Copy the **Baby Talk Nonsense Words reproducible (page 47)** and cut out the cards. Place the cards facedown in the center of a table.

2. Explain to students that when babies are learning to talk, their words usually contain short vowels and make no sense to anyone but other babies. Challenge students to figure out this amazing baby language! Invite each student to take a turn choosing a card from the pile and saying the nonsense word. Students will need to use their decoding skills since these "words" are not really ones they have seen or read before.

3. If a student decodes the nonsense word correctly and identifies the short-vowel sound, give him or her a token. (Use any type of small item, such as beans, paper clips, candy, or mini-plastic pacifiers from a craft store.)

4. The player with the most tokens at the end of the game is the "Baby Talk" champion.

5. For an extra challenge, invite students to invent long-vowel "baby talk" nonsense words. Encourage them to use their knowledge of long-vowel rules, such as *CVC*, silent *e*, and two vowels together.

978-1-4129-5821-9

Baby Talk Nonsense Words

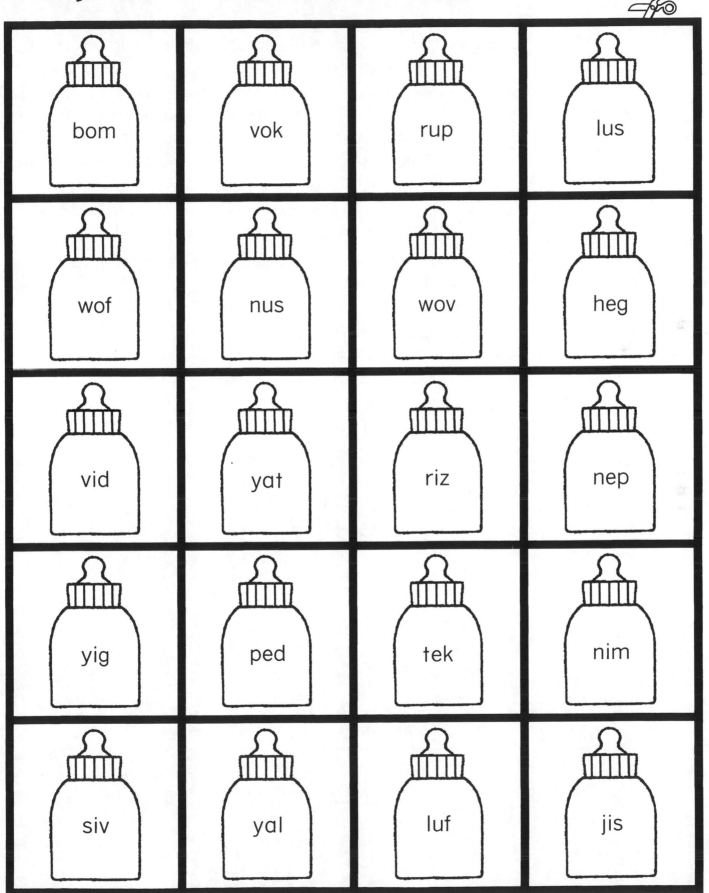

bom	vok	rup	lus
wof	nus	wov	heg
vid	yat	riz	nep
yig	ped	tek	nim
siv	yal	luf	jis

Dodge It

In this activity, students distinguish between short- and long-vowel sounds. Students need to listen carefully to the words you "throw" at them in order to identify the vowel sound.

1. Invite students to stand behind their desks. Explain that you will say a word to each student. If the word you say has a long-vowel sound, the student will remain standing and "catch" the word by chanting the long-vowel sound three times, such as: /ā/ /ā/ /ā/.

2. If the word has a short-vowel sound, the student will "dodge" the word by saying the short-vowel sound only once and ducking down to avoid being "hit" by the word.

3. The following word lists contain both short- and long-vowel sounds. Invite students to listen closely as you say each word to determine if they need to catch or dodge the word.

Long and Short A

came	stay	razor	fan	sad
cap	same	than	brat	man
bait	rat	drain	frame	place

Long and Short E

easy	men	jet	team	relief
beach	teacher	better	message	bleed
red	tent	each	effort	bean

Long and Short I

hid	bridge	glide	middle	style
pit	bride	chicken	tiny	brim
slide	chime	grime	mile	ride

Long and Short O

slow	stop	chop	shoulder	over
motor	grown	frog	pot	coal
hot	broad	clover	drove	croak

Long and Short U

tuba	bugle	cup	rug	bug
cuddle	juice	suit	hungry	stub
true	butter	rubber	lunch	cute

978-1-4129-5821-9

Nail It Down

For students, the hardest part of learning about long-vowel words is remembering the different spellings and knowing when to use them. In this activity, students work on "nailing down" different long *a* spellings.

1. Make a copy of the **Long *A* Nails reproducible (page 51)**. Laminate the page, if desired, and cut out the nails. Place the nails in the center of a work surface so all students can see them and are able to reach them.

2. Explain that you will read a word with a long *a* sound to each student. Refer to the **Long-Vowel Word Lists reproducible (page 50)**. After you read the word, the player uses a plastic hammer to "nail" the correct long *a* spelling for that word by hitting the corresponding nail on the table with the hammer.

3. If the student nails the correct spelling, he or she earns a point. If the student is unable to nail the correct spelling, he or she passes the hammer to the next player and earns no points. The student who has the most points at the end of the game wins.

4. Repeat the activity using the other long-vowel sound spellings on the **Long *E*, *I*, *O*, *U* Nails reproducibles (pages 52–55)**.

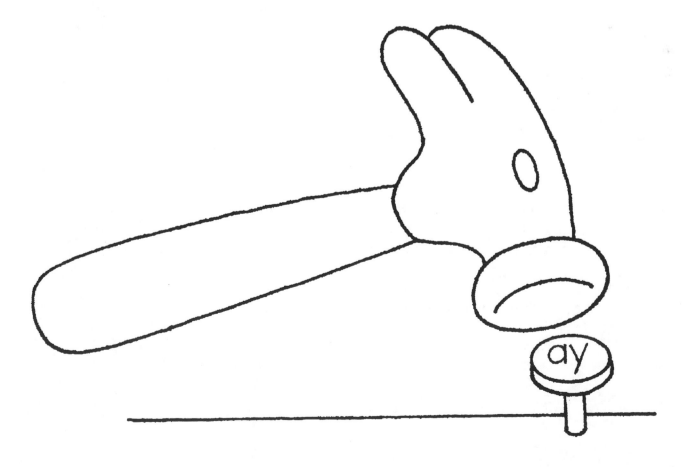

Long-Vowel Word Lists

LONG A SOUND SPELLINGS

a	a__e	ai	ay
apron	face	rain	say
tomato	name	chain	play
radio	shape	paid	stay
paper	state	mail	day

LONG E SOUND SPELLINGS

e	e__e	ee	__y	ie
female	athlete	free	candy	achieve
prefix	trapeze	sweet	funny	piece
secret	here	teeth	lucky	retrieve
equal	complete	knee	happy	relief

LONG I SOUND SPELLINGS

i	i__e	ie	__y	igh
title	ride	pie	sly	bright
tiny	write	tie	cry	might
pilot	mile	lie	sky	fright
icy	white	tied	why	sigh

LONG O SOUND SPELLINGS

o	o__e	ow	oe	oa
zero	home	snow	toe	toad
cargo	rose	elbow	doe	loaf
volcano	phone	grow	aloe	oatmeal
ocean	globe	blown	goes	foam

LONG U SOUND SPELLINGS

u	u__e	ue	ew
human	cube	glue	cashew
menu	tune	tissue	stew
music	flute	statue	dew
humor	tube	issue	jewel
uniform	rude	blue	nephew
bugle	June	hue	knew

Long A Nails

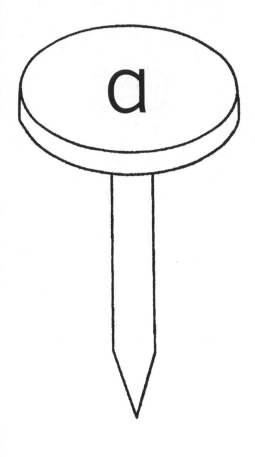

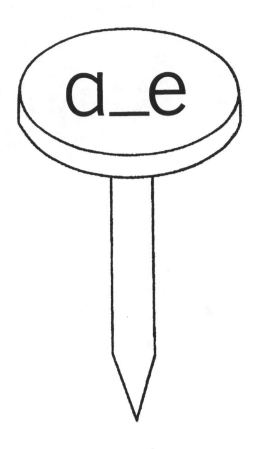

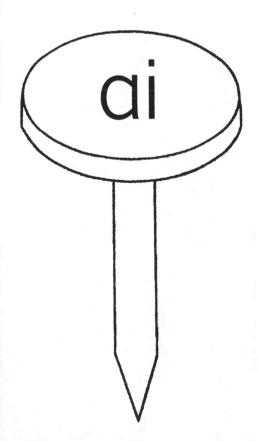

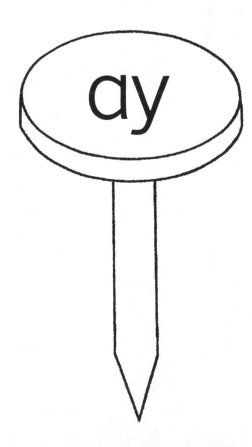

Long E Nails

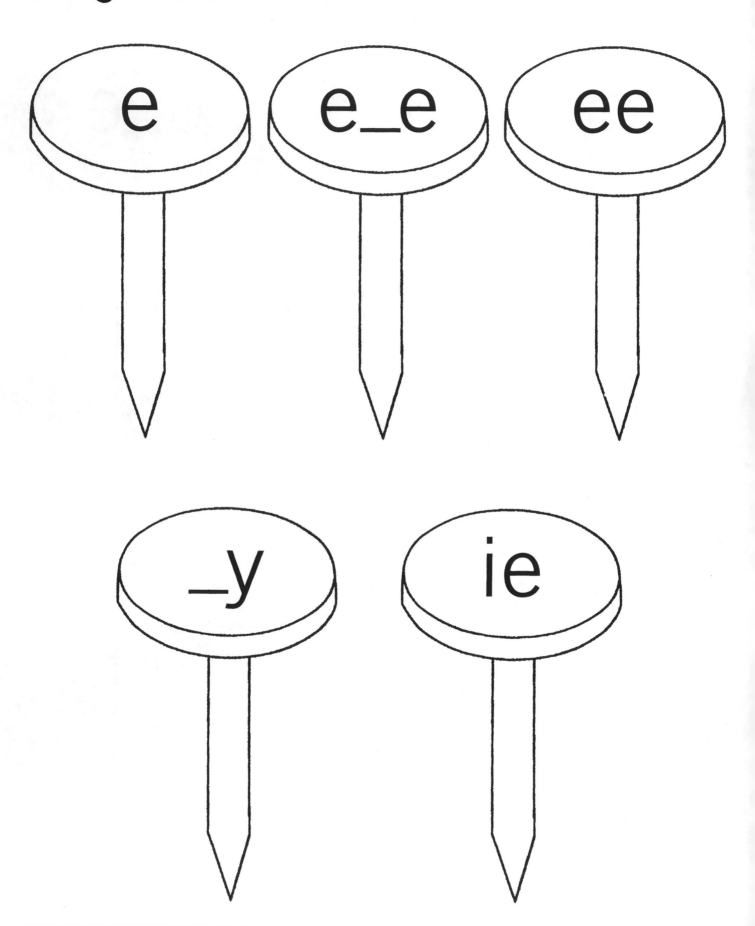

Long / Nails

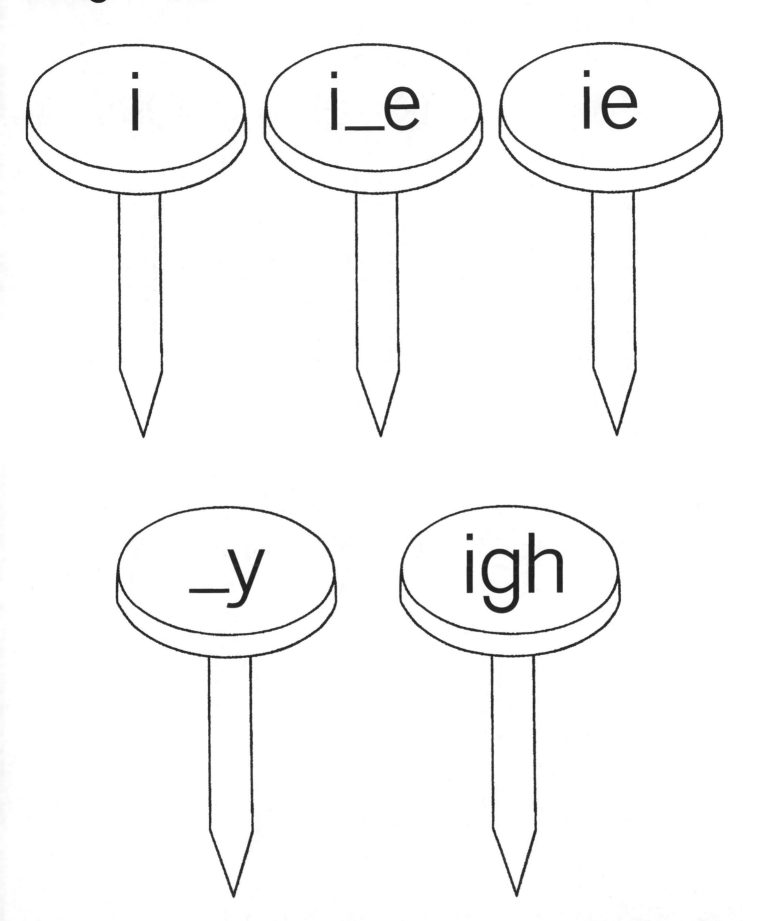

Long *O* Nails

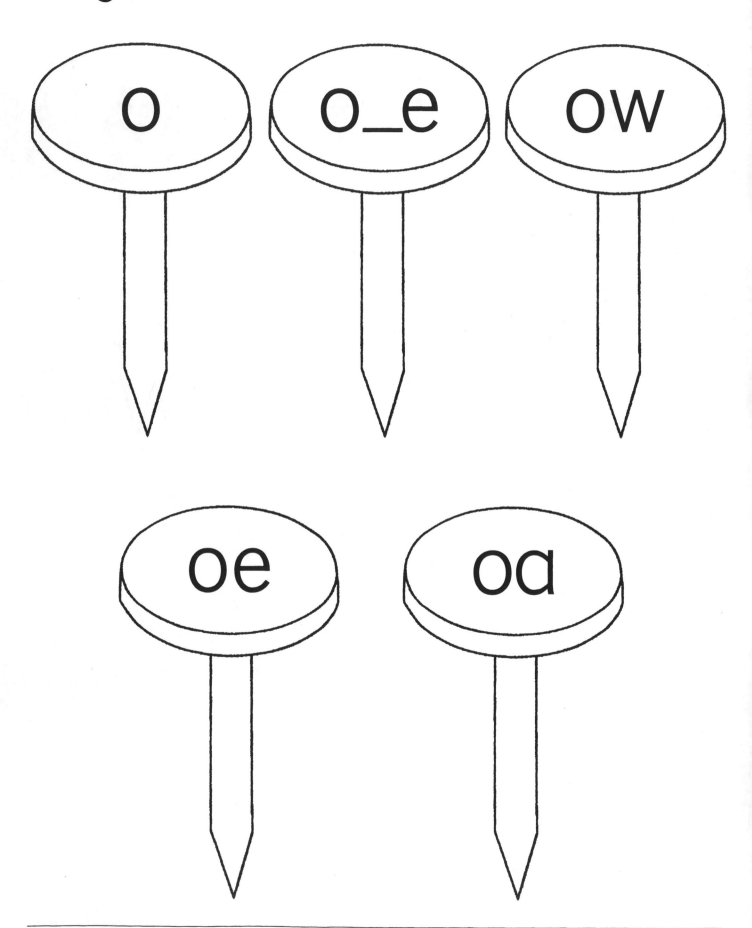

Long *U* Nails

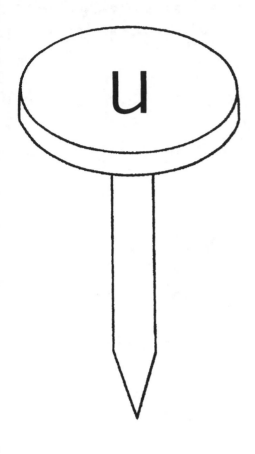

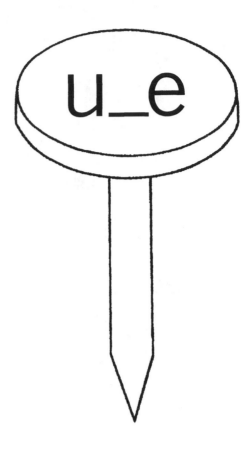

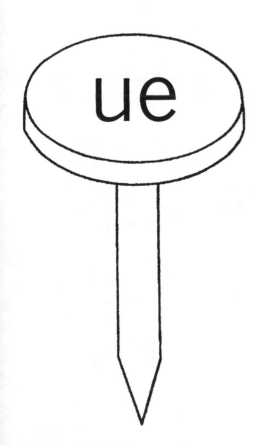

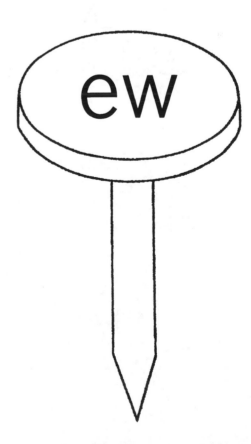

Vacationing Vowels

1. Explain to students that the long vowels are planning to go on a long, long vacation together but are in a terrible disagreement. Then read aloud the "Vacationing Vowels" story.

Vacationing Vowels

"Hey, hey, hey!" said Long **A**. "Today's the day we're on our way. Today we take off for the bay, I say!"

"Hee, hee, hee!" said Long **E**. "I really don't think I agree. We are leaving for the beach, you see!"

"My, my, my!" said Long **I**. "In a while we'll be on the isle. Then we can lie around and smile!"

"Oh, no, no!" said Long **O**. "It's to the ocean we will go!"

Then Long **U** boomed, "You, you, you! It's true! It's true! You really don't make all the rules! In a different universe is where I'll be, because this arguing angers me!"

2. Tell students that the long vowels are all very upset with each other, so they have decided to take separate vacations. Long *A* is taking a trip to the b**ay**. Long *E* is going to the b**ea**ch, and Long *I* is resting at the **i**sle. Long *O* is going to the **o**cean. Long *U* is heading to the edge of the **u**niverse, as far from the others as possible. But somehow in this vacation mess, their luggage gets all mixed together. The long vowels need help getting their luggage back to the proper destination.

3. Make several copies of the **Vacationing Vowels game board** and **Long A, E, I, O, U Luggage Cards reproducibles (pages 57–62)**. Cut out the cards. Give each group of six students a game board and set of Luggage Cards. Invite five players from each group to choose a vowel vacation path on the group's game board. Let the sixth player in each group be the "travel guide." Direct each travel guide to draw a card from the stack and read it aloud, stressing the vowel sound. The player in each group with the matching vowel sound colors in one space on his or her vacation path.

4. Play continues with the travel guide reading the words until one player reaches his or her vacation destination.

Name _____ Date _____

Vacationing Vowels

Universe									Start

Ocean									Start

Isle									Start

Beach									Start

Bay									Start

Long A Luggage Cards

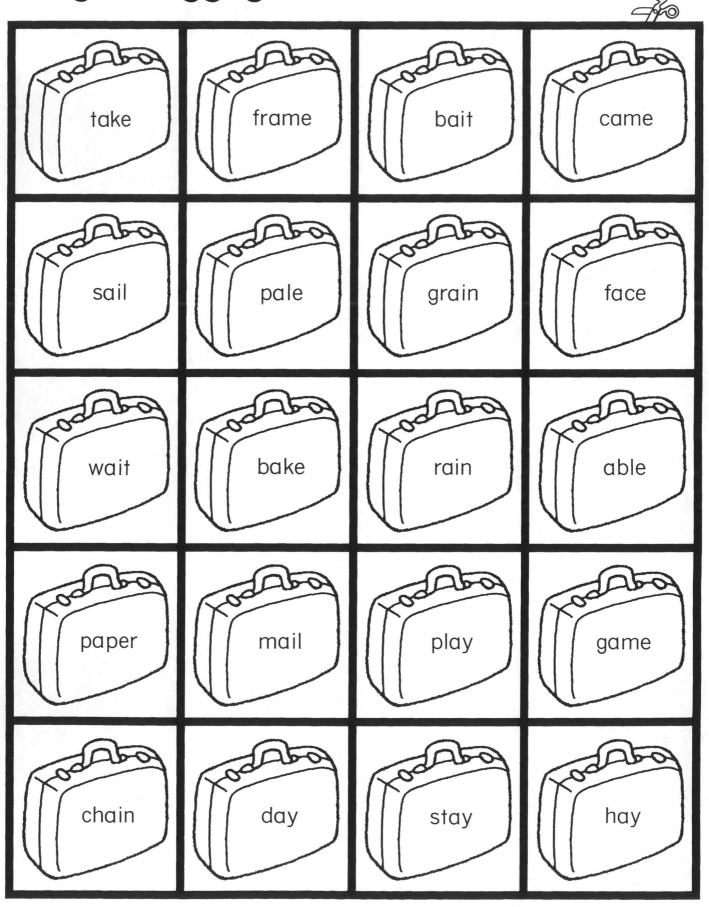

take | frame | bait | came
sail | pale | grain | face
wait | bake | rain | able
paper | mail | play | game
chain | day | stay | hay

Long *E* Luggage Cards

deer	green	bean	me
here	free	read	teeth
teach	knee	seen	clean
seal	sweet	she	equal
please	sneeze	steep	sleep

Long / Luggage Cards

bite	try	cry	ice
size	fries	five	shy
tight	fire	lie	white
file	right	dive	high
hive	smile	light	drive

Reproducible 978-1-4129-5821-9 • © Corwin Press

Long *O* Luggage Cards

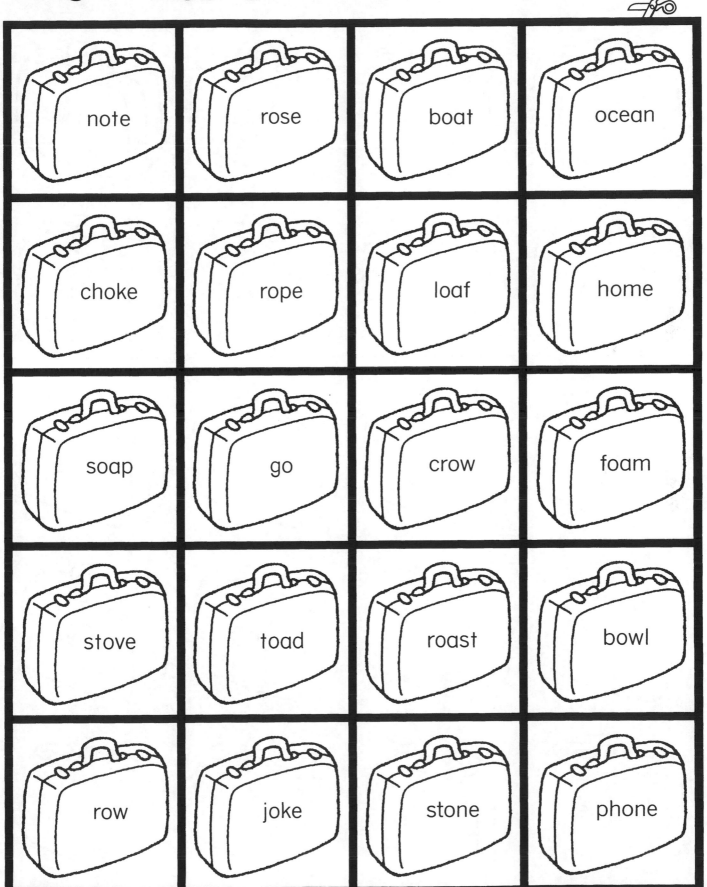

note	rose	boat	ocean
choke	rope	loaf	home
soap	go	crow	foam
stove	toad	roast	bowl
row	joke	stone	phone

Long *U* Luggage Cards

cube	juice	tube	chew
brew	prune	cute	hue
June	flute	knew	shoe
tuna	blue	glue	new
Sue	rude	fuse	use

CHAPTER 3

Blast Off with Blends and Digraphs

Draw It

All young artists can hop onboard for a fast-paced game of "Draw It," which is played like the popular game *Pictionary*® (a registered trademark of Pictionary Incorporated).

1. Divide the class into two or three teams. Make a copy of the **Blends Word Cards reproducibles (pages 64–65)**. Cut out the cards and place them facedown in a stack.

2. Direct the first player on the first team to choose a card and read it silently. Set a timer for one minute. Invite the player to illustrate the word on chart paper for his or her teammates to guess.

3. If the team can correctly identify the word and its initial consonant blend before the timer goes off, the team keeps the card and earns one point. If the team is unable to guess the word, give the other teams a chance to "steal" the point by making a correct guess.

4. Play continues until all team members have a chance to show off their artwork and their knowledge of blends.

Snap It Up

1. Place students in small groups. Make a copy of the **Snap and Match Blends Cards reproducibles (pages 66–68)** for each group. Cut out the cards. Choose the cards that represent the blends you want to reinforce, such as *r* or *l* blends. Be sure that for each beginning blend there is a matching picture card.

2. Have each group spread out their cards facedown in a grid pattern on a table. Let students take turns turning over two cards at a time. If the two cards match, the player keeps the cards. For example, if a player turns over the *br* card and the broom picture, a match is made. The player keeps the matching pair and takes another turn. If the player does not make a match, he or she turns the cards facedown again and the next player takes a turn.

3. The game continues until all card pairs have been matched. The player in each group with the most pairs wins.

Blends Word Cards

blanket	blouse	bread	bride
bridge	clock	clouds	crab
crib	crown	dragon	drum
flamingo	flashlight	frame	frog
grapes	grass	planets	plate

Reproducible   978-1-4129-5821-9 • © Corwin Press

Blends Word Cards

plug	pretzel	princess	skate
skunk	sled	slide	spider
spoon	square	squirrel	stamp
star	stove	stump	swim
swing	train	treasure	truck

Snap and Match Blends Cards

br___	___idge	fr___	___ies
cr___	___own	br___	___oom
dr___	___ess	dr___	___um
pr___	___incess	tr___	___ain
gr___	___apes	cr___	___ab

Snap and Match Blends Cards

cl___	___own	sl___	___ide
bl___	___ouse	cl___	___ouds
gl___	___obe	bl___	___ocks
fl___	___ower	gl___	___oves
pl___	___ant	fl___	___ashlight

Snap and Match Blends Cards

sp___	___aghetti	sk___	___ates
sn___	___ail	sp___	___oon
sk___	___unk	sm___	___oke
st___	___ar	sl___	___ed
sw___	___ing	sq___	___uirrel

Clickety-Clack

For this whole-class activity, students "chug, chug, chug" along as they generate words that start with the beginning blend identified in the chant.

1. Ask students to sit in a circle. Announce a target blend to complete the chant below. Invite students to pass a small toy train around the circle as you chant the "Clickety-Clack Song."

Clickety-Clack Song

> Clickety-clack, clickety-clack,
>
> Our train is traveling 'round the track.
>
> Clickety-clack, clickety-clack,
>
> Let's say a ____ word, or we send it back!

2. When the chant is done, the student holding the train must say a word that begins with the blend. For example, if the target blend is *sp*, a student might say: *Spider.*

3. If the student is unable to say a word with the matching beginning blend, direct students to send the train back to the "station" (back to you). Make the game more challenging by periodically completing the chant with a new blend.

Tricky Top Hat

1. Place students in small groups. Make a copy of the **Tricky Top Hat Cards reproducibles (pages 70–73)** for each group. Cut out the cards and place the beginning blends (onsets) in one pile and the ending sounds (rimes) in another pile.

2. Have the first player in each group choose one card from each of the piles. Instruct the player to say the beginning blend and word ending together. If the two sounds form a word, he or she should say: *Hocus pocus!* and then the word. For example, if a player draws the *bl* card and the *ack* card, he or she should say: *Hocus pocus,* **black**. Any player who makes a match keeps the card pair.

3. If a player draws two cards that do not make a word, he or she should return the cards to the appropriate piles. The player in each group with the most card pairs wins.

Tricky Top Hat Cards (Onsets)

tr___	tr___	cr___	cr___
dr___	dr___	fr___	fr___
gr___	gr___	pr___	pr___
br___	br___	cl___	cl___
bl___	bl___	gl___	gl___

Reproducible   978-1-4129-5821-9 • © *Corwin Press*

Tricky Top Hat Cards (Onsets)

fl___	fl___	pl___	pl___
sl___	sl___	sl___	sp___
sp___	sn___	sn___	sk___
sk___	st___	st___	sw___
sw___	str___	str___	str___

Tricky Top Hat Cards (Rimes)

___ack   ___ail   ___ain   ___ake

___am   ___ame   ___amp   ___ank

___ank   ___ap   ___ash   ___ash

___ate   ___aw   ___ay   ___ed

___eed   ___ice   ___ick   ___ue

Tricky Top Hat Cards (Rimes)

___ide	___ight	___ill	___ing
___ing	___ink	___ip	___oat
___ock	___ock	___oke	___op
___op	___ove	___own	___uff
___ug	___ump	___unk	___unk

Flip-Flop Toss

1. Draw a 16-square grid on a large plastic tablecloth. Write a beginning blend in each square using the suggested blends on this page or any that you choose to reinforce.

2. Have students gather around the grid. Choose a student to be the first player. Have the player gently toss a flip-flop onto a square in the grid. Ask him or her to say a word that begins with the blend in that square.

3. Write the word on chart paper and underline the beginning blend. For example, if the flip-flop lands on the *dr* blend, the player might say: *Drain.* Write *drain* on the chart paper and underline *dr*. Invite students to brainstorm other words that begin with the *dr* blend (see suggestions below). Add the words to the chart.

4. Invite the next player to toss a flip-flop onto the grid and use the blend to create a word. Continue the game, creating a list of words for each blend.

gr	**bl**	**pl**	**sw**	**st**	**sp**
grab	bloom	place	sweet	stain	space
graph	black	please	switch	stage	spot
grass	blink	planet	swam	stamp	speak
great	blame	plastic	swept	start	spell
green	blouse	plenty	swing	store	spin

pr	**tr**	**br**	**cl**	**dr**	**fl**
practice	trace	branch	claw	drip	flag
present	treat	bridge	clam	drink	flower
print	trick	brick	clay	dress	flute
pretend	trim	bride	clock	drain	flood
pretty	tree	bright	cloud	dragon	flavor

sm	**fr**	**sl**	**cr**
small	free	sleeve	crab
smart	from	sleep	cream
smell	front	slipper	crow
smile	fruit	sled	crash
smooth	frog	slug	cracker

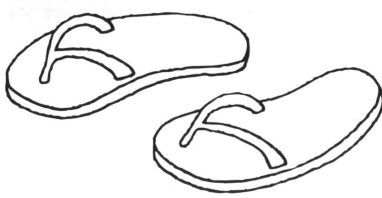

978-1-4129-5821-9

Three's a Crowd

1. Give each student a copy of the **Three's a Crowd game board reproducible (page 76)**. Invite students to play this game in pairs. Make copies of the **Consonant Digraphs reproducible (page 77)** and cut out the cards. Give each pair of students a set of cards and have them place the cards facedown in a pile.

2. Explain that the object of the game is for players to complete a row of words using the same consonant digraph. The first player chooses a card, identifies the sound, and writes a word that begins with that digraph on a line on his or her game board. For example, a player might draw the *ch* card and write the word *chin*.

3. If a player is unable to think of a word for the digraph, he or she loses a turn. Continue to play until one player completes a row of three words for a single digraph.

Treasure Chest Hunt

1. Give each group of three or four students a copy of the **Treasure Chest Hunt game board reproducible (page 78)**. Give every student a game piece to place on the starting line. Copy the **Gold Coins reproducible (page 79)** on gold or yellow cardstock. Cut out the coins and place them in a box decorated to look like a treasure chest.

2. Explain to students that many years ago, pirates sailed the seas to distant lands, searching for hidden treasure. Pirates often had maps that showed where the treasure was buried. Tell students that their game board is a map to buried treasure.

3. Invite the first player in each group to draw a coin from the treasure chest and move to the first corresponding space on the game board. He or she must then say a word that begins with that digraph.

4. Invite players to take turns drawing coins and moving along the game board. The first player in each group to reach the treasure chest wins.

Three's a Crowd

Directions: Choose a letter card. Write a word that begins with those letters on a line below. How fast you can fill all three lines in a row?

Consonant Digraphs

ch___	th___	sh___	wh___
ch___	th___	sh___	wh___
ch___	th___	sh___	wh___
ch___	th___	sh___	wh___
ch___	th___	sh___	wh___

Treasure Chest Hunt

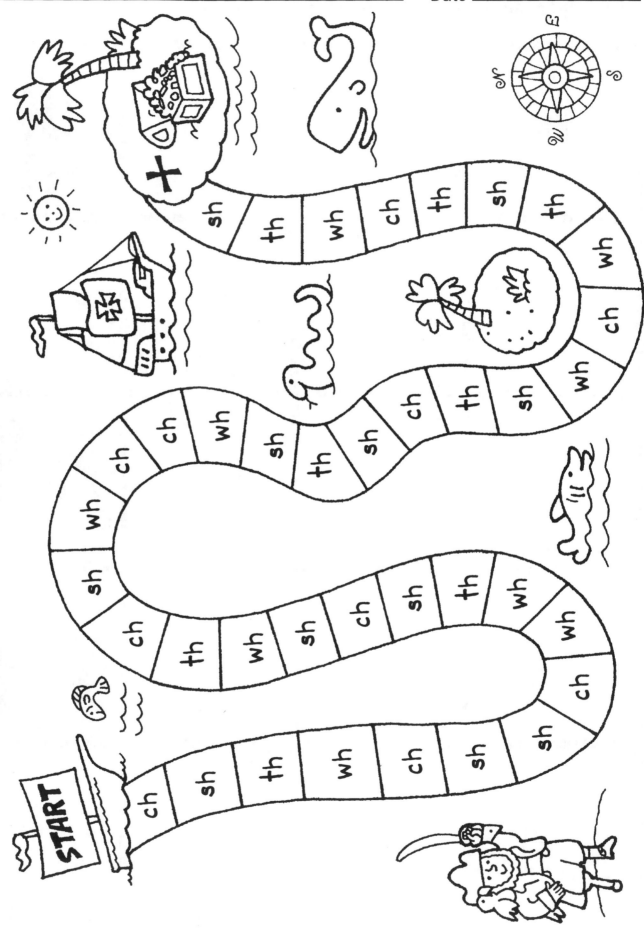

Gold Coins

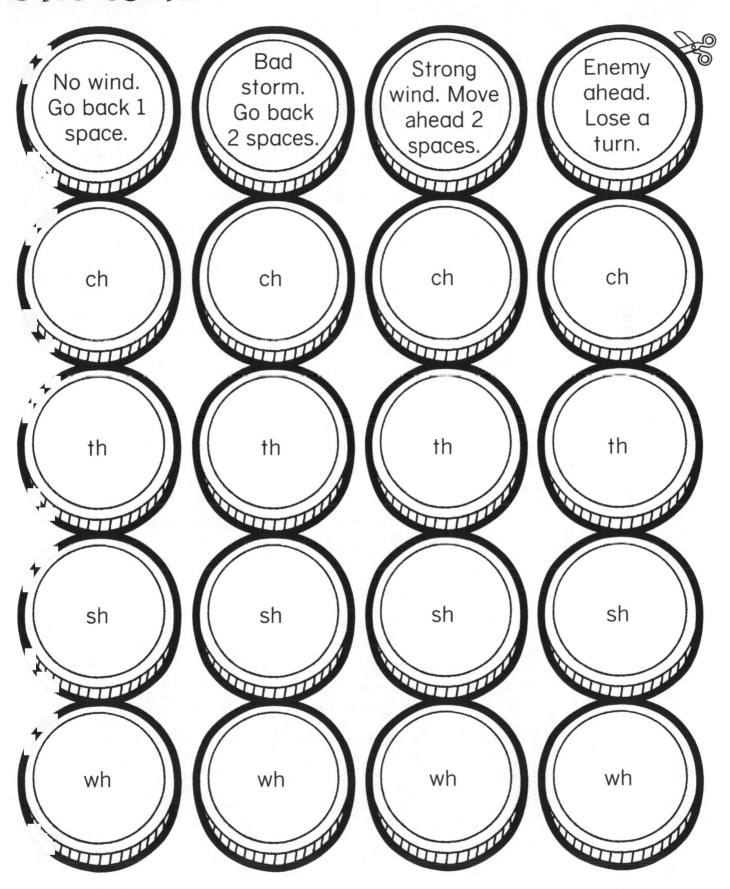

No wind. Go back 1 space.	Bad storm. Go back 2 spaces.	Strong wind. Move ahead 2 spaces.	Enemy ahead. Lose a turn.
ch	ch	ch	ch
th	th	th	th
sh	sh	sh	sh
wh	wh	wh	wh

CHAPTER 4

Sight Word Satellite

Snap or Steal

Sight words comprise a large percentage of the words students encounter in their daily reading. Being able to recognize them at a glance improves both fluency and comprehension. The 220 sight words on the **Dolch Sight Words reproducible (page 81)** are divided by grade level into five lists.

1. Choose the sight words you wish to reinforce. Write one word in each of the boxes on the **Word Card Template reproducibles (pages 82–83)** to make game cards. Place students in small groups. For each group, make a copy of both card reproducibles on colored copy paper. The color will prevent students from being able to see the words through the backside. Cut out the cards. Give each group a set of cards and have them place their cards facedown in a pile.

2. Invite one player from each group to draw the top card and read the word. If the player reads the word correctly, he or she keeps the card. If the player reads the word incorrectly, he or she must place the card on the bottom of the pile.

3. If a player draws a *Snap* card, he or she loses all cards. The other players shout: *Snap!* as the player returns all of his or her cards to the bottom of the pile.

4. If a player draws a *Steal* card, he or she can steal a card from any other player.

5. Tell students that no matter how many cards they collect or lose throughout the game, they can still be the winner. To determine the winner, roll a die. The student holding the same number of cards as the number on the die is the winner. If the die lands on six, all students with six or more cards win!

6. Play the game on another day using a new list of words.

978-1-4129-5821-9

Dolch Sight Words

Pre-Primer		Primer		First Grade		Second Grade		Third Grade	
a	play	all	out	after	once	always	right	about	never
and	red	am	please	again	open	around	sing	better	only
away	run	are	pretty	an	over	because	sit	bring	own
big	said	at	ran	any	put	been	sleep	carry	pick
blue	see	ate	ride	as	round	before	tell	clean	seven
can	the	be	saw	ask	some	best	their	cut	shall
come	three	black	say	by	stop	both	these	done	show
down	to	brown	she	could	take	buy	those	draw	six
find	two	but	so	every	thank	call	upon	drink	small
for	up	came	soon	fly	them	cold	us	eight	start
funny	we	did	that	from	then	does	use	fall	ten
go	where	do	there	give	think	don't	very	far	today
help	yellow	eat	they	giving	walk	fast	wash	full	together
here	you	four	this	had	were	first	which	got	try
I		get	too	has	when	five	why	grow	warm
in		good	under	her		found	wish	hold	
is		have	want	him		gave	work	hot	
it		he	was	his		goes	would	hurt	
jump		into	well	how		green	write	if	
little		like	went	just		its	your	keep	
look		must	what	know		made		kind	
make		new	white	let		many		laugh	
me		no	who	live		off		light	
my		now	will	may		or		long	
not		on	with	of		pull		much	
one		our	yes	old		read		myself	

Word Card Template

Steal!

Steal!

Snap!

Snap!

978-1-4129-5821-9 • © Corwin Press

Word Card Template

Wrapping Up Words

1. Select words you want to reinforce from the Dolch Sight Words reproducible (page 81). Write one word in each blank card on the Word Card Template reproducibles. Reproduce the sight words and cut out the cards.

2. Use colorful wrapping paper to decorate a simple box that contains small incentives, such as candies, stickers, or pencils. Tape one word card to each side of the wrapped gift box.

3. Divide the class into two groups. Ask the first group to sit in a circle. Invite each student in the second group to stand behind a seated student.

4. Discuss with students the excitement everyone feels about opening gifts. Remind them that part of the excitement is the surprise of not knowing what is inside the package.

5. Tell students that they are going to review sight words by playing a game. Tell them that while music is playing, they will pass a gift box around the circle. When the music stops, the student holding the box will point to a word on the box, then say the word, spell the word, and use the word in a sentence.

6. Play music and invite the seated students to pass the box around the circle. Stop the music at random. If the student holding the box when the music stops says, spells, and uses the word correctly, then the student standing behind him or her changes places and joins those seated in the circle.

7. Continue playing until each standing student is seated in the circle. Then tell students that they did a great job and it's time to wrap up the game and unwrap the gift! Choose a student to unwrap the box to reveal the gifts hidden inside. Then hand out the treats.

8. Repeat the game on another day using different sight word cards taped to the gift box.

978-1-4129-5821-9

Word Detectives

1. Make several copies of the Word Card Template reproducibles (pages 82–83) and cut out the blank cards.

2. Invite each student to think of a sight word that contains three or more letters. Have students hold up the same number of fingers as there are letters in their words. For example, a student who chose a four-letter word would hold up four fingers.

3. When all students are holding up the corresponding number of fingers, give each student that number of blank cards.

4. Have students write each letter of their word on a separate blank card and place the cards in an envelope. Ask students to write their name on the front of the envelope.

5. Collect all of the completed envelopes and hide them around the classroom.

6. Explain to students that they are going to be word detectives. Their job is to search the room to find the lost sight words. Invite each student to search for any envelope and return to his or her seat after finding one. Once all students are seated, have each "detective" take the letters out of the envelope and put the word together letter by letter.

7. Invite the class to repeat the "Word Detective Chant" with you.

Word Detective Chant

Words, words all around,
What's the word that you have found?

8. Choose one student to say and spell his or her word and then return the letters to the envelope. Repeat the chant as a class and invite a new student to say and spell his or her word and place the letters back in the envelope. Continue until all students have had a chance to say and spell their sight words.

CHAPTER 5

Compound Constellations

Compound Crashers

1. Make copies of the **Compound Crasher Cars reproducibles (pages 87–90)**. Notice that the cars facing right on page 87 and those facing left on page 88 pair up to create compound words. The right-facing cars on page 89 and the left-facing cards on page 90 also match up to create compound words. Choose one group of Compound Crasher Cars and cut them out. Place one set of cars faceup on one side of a table. Place the other set of cars faceup on the other side of the table.

2. Tell students to pretend to drive through Compound City in search of compound words. Remind them that a compound word is a word made up of two smaller words.

3. Choose one student to go first. Ask the player to choose a car from one side of the table and read the word aloud. Then challenge the player to choose a car from the other side of the table and "crash" the two words together to make a new word. Invite the player to say the compound word aloud.

4. If the word is a compound word, invite all students to shout: *Crash!* and repeat the compound word together.

5. Continue to play the game until each student has had a chance to make a compound word "car crash."

6. Play again on a different day using the other set of Compound Crasher Cars.

Compound Crasher Cars

foot	snow	butter
candle	lady	book
rail	door	sail
bed	earth	sand

Compound Crasher Cars

ball

flake

fly

stick

bug

bag

road

knob

boat

room

worm

paper

978-1-4129-5821-9 • © Corwin Press

Compound Crasher Cars

hot

race

cross

down

tea

news

pop

cow

drive

half

lip

cup

Compound Crasher Cars

dog

track

walk

stairs

pot

paper

corn

boy

way

time

stick

cake

978-1-4129-5821-9 • © Corwin Press

Come Pound the Word

1. Use a permanent marker to divide a shower curtain into an even number of equal squares to make a class game board. The number of squares will depend on how many words you would like to use.

2. Choose a few compound words that you would like students to review. Using a black erasable marker, write the first part of each compound word in the center of half the squares. Choose a different color marker and write the second part of each compound word in the remaining squares.

3. After you have written a word in each square, tell students that they are going to "come *pound* the words." Place students in two lines. Let the first student in one line use a toy hammer to pound a word on the game board while saying it aloud. Invite the first student from the second line to find a word, which when combined with the first word, will make a compound word. Have that student pound the word with the toy hammer and say the word aloud.

4. Once both players have pounded a word, invite the class to say the "Come-Pound Word Chant" to combine the two words into a compound word.

Come-Pound Word Chant

*Here are two words that we found: **bed**, **time**.*

*Hammer together to make a compound: **bedtime**.*

5. Continue the game until all students have had an opportunity to "come pound a word."

Sample Compound Words

airplane	bullfrog	dogcatcher	football	playroom
armpit	buttercup	doghouse	halftime	popcorn
backpack	catfish	doorknob	handbag	racetrack
bagpipe	checkup	doorway	herself	rainbow
barnyard	clockwise	downstairs	himself	sailboat
baseball	copycat	driveway	hotdog	sandpaper
bathroom	countdown	earmuff	inside	snowflake
bedtime	cowboy	earthworm	ladybug	sunflower
bobcat	cowgirl	eyebrow	lipstick	teapot
breakfast	crosswalk	eyelid	newspaper	timeout
briefcase	cupcake	firefighter	outside	upstairs
bubblegum	daytime	flashlight	pigtail	vineyard

Toss a Word

1. Invite students sit in a circle or at their desks. Choose one student to go first. Have that player shout out a compound word and toss a beach ball to another player. Have the player who catches the ball shout out another compound word and toss the ball again.

2. Students take turns tossing the ball and shouting out compound words. The game ends when one player cannot think of a new compound word or repeats one that has already been said.

3. To vary the game, have all players stand while playing. If they cannot think of a new compound word or repeat one, have them sit down. Continue playing to see who the is last one standing.

A Trip to Compound Country

1. Tell students to pretend they are going to go on a trip to Compound Country. They will need to think of compound words that name items that they want to bring with them. For example, a student might say: *I'm going on a trip to Compound Country. I'm going to take a* **goldfish**.

2. Choose a student to play first. Invite another student to repeat what the first player said and then add another compound item. The second student might say: *I'm going on a trip to Compound Country. I'm going to take a* **goldfish** *and a* **meatball**. Adapt the game for various grade levels and abilities by asking students to name just one new compound item rather than remembering all the items other students have named.

3. Continue playing to see how many compound items students can remember.

Crabby Compounds Bingo

1. Make a copy of the **Crabby Compounds reproducible (page 94)**. Cut out the cards.

2. Give each student a copy of the **Bingo Bed reproducible (page 95)** and a set of dried beans (pinto or navy) to use as game pieces. Explain to students that a group of compound words did not get enough sleep last night, so they are very crabby. The students' job is to get these crabby compounds back into bed so they can get a good night's sleep.

3. Choose a compound word card and read it aloud to students. Invite students to write the word on any square of their Bingo Bed. Place the word card in a bag. Continue drawing words and saying them aloud until students have written a word in each square on their Bingo Bed.

4. Be sure to place all the words that you call in the bag. As a signal to begin the game, invite students to chant the following: *Crabby compounds need to rest. When they wake, they'll be their best.*

5. Choose a word card from the bag and read it aloud. Direct each student to place a bean on that word on his or her Bingo Bed. When a player covers three words in a row, he or she shouts: *Crabby compounds, time to wake up!*

Compound Connection

1. Write various compound words on separate sentence strips. Color-code the words. Write the first word in each compound in one color and the second word in each compound in another color.

2. Cut the compound words in half, separating the two words into individual word cards.

3. Give each student a card. Invite students to find a friend who has a word (printed in a different color) that, when combined with their word, makes a compound word.

Crabby Compounds

baseball	birthday	campfire
catfish	doorbell	fireplace
mailbox	pancake	popcorn
rainbow	sandbox	scarecrow
starfish	wallpaper	wheelchair

Bingo Bed

References

Adams, M. J. (1990). *Beginning to read.* Cambridge, MA: MIT Press.

Antrim, J. (2001). *Summaries of test scores at Eureka School.* Unpublished report, Eureka School, Rockwood School District, Eureka, MO.

Bond, G. L., & Dykstra, R. (1967). The cooperative research program in the first-grade reading instruction. *Reading Research Quarterly, 2*(4), 10–89.

Carter, S. C. (1999). *No excuses: Seven principles of low-income schools who set the standard for high achievement.* Washington, DC: Heritage Foundation.

Chall, J. S. (1983). *Learning to read: The great debate.* New York, NY: McGraw-Hill. (Original work published 1967.)

Chall, J. S. (1996). *Learning to read: The great debate.* Fort Worth, TX: Harcourt Brace.

Dobberteen, C. (2001). *Second annual Chase Change Award: Essay.* Unpublished paper, La Mesa Dale Elementary School, La Mesa, CA.

Ehri, L. C. (1998). Grapheme-phoneme knowledge is essential for learning to read words in English. In J. L. Metsala & L. C. Ehri (Eds.), *Word recognition in beginning literacy* (pp. 3–40). Hillsdale, NJ: Lawrence Erlbaum.

Foorman, B. R., Fletcher, J. M., Francis, D. J., Schatschneider, C. (2000). Response: Misrepresentation of research by other researchers. *Educational Research Research, 29*(6), 27–37.

Foorman, B. R., Fletcher, J. M., Francis, D. J., Schatschneider, C., & Mehta, P. (1998). The role of instruction in learning to read: Preventing reading failure in at-risk children. *Journal of Educational Psychology, 90*(1), 37–55.

Fry, E. B., Kress, J. E., & Fountoukidis, D. L. (1993). *The reading teacher's book of lists.* Paramus, NJ: Prentice Hall, Inc.

Hall, S. (2006). *I've dibel'd, now what?* Longmont, CO: Sopris West Educational Services.

King, S. R., & Torgesen, J. K. (2000). *Improving the effectiveness of reading instruction in one elementary school: A description of the process.* Unpublished manuscript.

Kollars, D. (1999, June 25). City schools improve in statewide reading, math tests. *Sacrameto Bee.* Retrieved July 20, 1999, from http://www.sacbee.com.

McEwan, E. K. (1998). *The principal's guide to raising reading achievement.* Thousand Oaks, CA: Corwin Press.

McEwan, E. K. (2001). *Raising reading achievement in middle and high schools: Five simple-to-follow strategies for principals.* Thousand Oaks, CA: Corwin Press.

McEwan, E. K. (2002). *Teach them all to read: Catching the kids who fall through the cracks.* Thousand Oaks, CA: Corwin Press.

National Reading Panel. (2000). *Report of the National Reading Panel: Teaching children to read: An evidence-based assessment of the scientific research literature on reading and its implications for reading instruction. Reports of the subgroups.* Rockville, MD: National Institute of Child Health and Human Development.

Reading academy: Alphabetic principle and phonics. (2005). Tallahassee, FL: Florida Center for Reading Research.

Snow, C. E., Burns, M. S., & Griffin, P. (Eds). (1998). *Preventing reading difficulties in young children.* Washington, DC: National Academy Press, Committee on the Prevention of Reading Difficulties in Young Children, Commission on Behavioral and Social Sciences and Education, National Research Council.

Young, S. (1994). *Scholastic rhyming dictionary.* New York, NY: Scholastic, Inc.

Printed in the United States
By Bookmasters